Contents

Any words appearing in bold, **like this**, are explained in the Glossary.

England

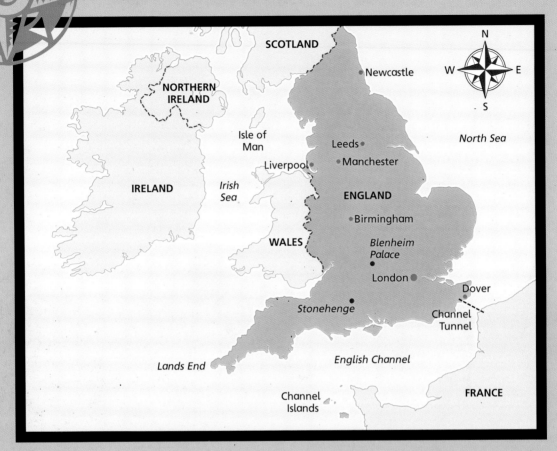

England is a country in the United Kingdom. It is also part of a group of islands called the British Isles. About 50 million people live in England.

Visit
ENGLAND

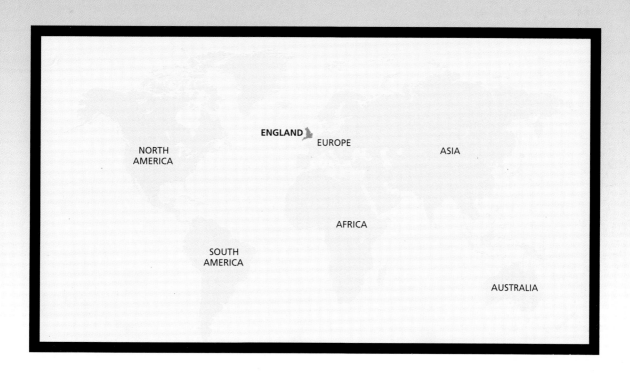

NORTH
AMERICA

ENGLAND EUROPE

ASIA

AFRICA

SOUTH
AMERICA

AUSTRALIA

Chris Oxlade and Anita Ganeri

www.heinemann.co.uk/library

Visit our website to find out more information about **Heinemann Library** books.

To order:

 Phone 44 (0) 1865 888066

 Send a fax to 44 (0) 1865 314091

 Visit the Heinemann Bookshop at www.heinemann.co.uk/library to browse our catalogue and order online.

First published in Great Britain by Heinemann Library, Halley Court, Jordan Hill, Oxford OX2 8EJ, part of Harcourt Education. Heinemann is a registered trademark of Harcourt Education Ltd.

Editorial: Nicole Irving and Georga Godwin
Design: Ron Kamen and StoreyBooks
Picture Research: Catherine Bevan and Ginny Stroud-Lewis
Production: Sévy Ribierre

Originated by Dot Gradations Ltd
Printed and bound in China by South China Printing Company

ISBN 0 431 08271 5 (hardback)
07 06 05 04 03
10 9 8 7 6 5 4 3 2 1

ISBN 0 431 08276 6 (paperback)
08 07 06 05 04
10 9 8 7 6 5 4 3 2 1

British Library Cataloguing in Publication Data
Oxlade, Chris and Ganeri, Anita
Visit England
914.2
A full catalogue record for this book is available from the British Library.

Acknowledgements
The Publishers would like to thank the following for permission to reproduce photographs: Collections/John Wender p. **26**; Collections/Paul Watts p. **25**; Collections/Ray Roberts p. **19**; Collections/Roger Scruton p. **13**; Corbis/Kim Sayer p. **20**; John Walmsley p. **22**; Peter Evans pp. **5**, **6**, **7**, **8**, **11**, **12**, **14**, **15**, **16**, **17**, **18**, **21**, **23**, **24**, **28**, **29**; Photodisc p. **9**; Trevor Clifford p. **10**; Trip/A. Tovy p. **27**.

Cover photograph of Stonehenge, reproduced with permission of Photodisc.

Every effort has been made to contact copyright holders of any material reproduced in this book. Any omissions will be rectified in subsequent printings if notice is given to the Publishers.

The **capital** city of England is called London. It is built along the River Thames. The buildings on the right-hand riverbank are called the Houses of Parliament.

Land

Most of the land in England is quite flat. It is divided up into fields, with **hedges** between them. Farmers raise animals or grow crops in the fields.

England has a long **coastline**. In the south and west, the coastline can be rocky, with steep cliffs. The east coast is often flat, with beaches and **mud flats**.

Landmarks

This is Blenheim Palace in central England. There are many **stately homes** like this in the English countryside. You can visit many of them and look around inside.

This circle of stones is called Stonehenge. People began building Stonehenge about 5000 years ago, dragging each stone into place. They may have **worshipped** the Sun here.

Homes

Most English people live in towns
and cities. Many live in streets of
semi-detached houses like these.
More families own their own homes
than **rent** them.

In most towns in England, there are streets of houses joined together in long rows. They are called **terraced** houses. Lots of these have a small garden at the back.

Food

This is a **traditional** English cooked breakfast. It is bacon, sausages, tomatoes, mushrooms, egg, fried bread and baked beans. Not many people eat this every day!

There are many restaurants in England that serve food from other countries of the world. Indian dishes, such as **curries** and spicy pickles, are very popular.

Clothes

When they are relaxing at home or out playing with their friends, young people in England wear comfortable clothes like T-shirts, jeans and sportswear.

Most children wear a **uniform** when they are at school. In some schools children must wear jackets and ties, like the boys here. In other schools the uniform is more casual.

Work

Millions of people in England travel into a town or city every day to work. Some drive or cycle, but many more go by bus or train.

More than 15 million people from other
countries visit England every year.
About one in twenty English people
work in jobs that have something to
do with **tourism**.

Transport

Buses, trams and underground trains carry people around England's city centres. This is the main bus station in Liverpool, where all the city's buses start and finish their journeys.

This train carries people between London, France and Belgium. The train goes through the Channel Tunnel. This runs under the sea between England and France.

Language

Most people in England speak English.
In different parts of the country
people speak with different **accents**.
People in some areas even have their
own words for things.

Many people move to England from other countries. They speak different languages. In towns and cities in England, they can buy newspapers written in their own languages.

School

In England, children start school
when they are four or five. They must
go to school until they are sixteen.
This is a **primary school** classroom.

These children go to a primary school
in a country village. When they are
eleven, they will travel every day to
a larger school in the nearest town.

Free time

In England children enjoy playing and watching sports such as cricket, football, tennis and netball. Cricket, tennis and football were first played in England.

People enjoy going **sightseeing** at the weekend and during school holidays. There are many **stately homes**, beaches and beautiful parts of the countryside to visit.

Celebrations

Guy Fawkes tried to blow up the Houses of Parliament on 5 November 1605, almost 400 years ago. People light bonfires and set off fireworks to celebrate Guy Fawkes Night.

The Notting Hill Carnival takes place
in August. People dress up in fantastic
costumes and parade through Notting
Hill, a part of London.

The Arts

England has many art galleries.
They show paintings, **sculptures** and
other works of art. This gallery in
Liverpool has paintings by famous
artists, such as Turner and Hockney.

England has many theatres. This is the Globe Theatre in London. It is a copy of the theatre where William Shakespeare's plays were first performed, 400 years ago.

Factfile

Name	England is part of the United Kingdom of Great Britain and Northern Ireland.
Capital	The capital city is London.
Language	English is the official language of England.
Population	About 50 million people live in England.
Money	In England, and all the other countries in the United Kingdom, the money is called pounds sterling (£). There are 100 pence in the pound.
Religion	The official Christian church in England is called the Church of England. There are several other churches, too. There are also many Muslims, Jews, Hindus and Sikhs in England.
Products	England produces medicines, fibres and textiles, electronics, cars, parts for planes, household goods, fruit and vegetables and animals for food. Finance and tourism are also important.

Words you can learn

North East (Geordie)	tatie	potato
	why-aye	of course
London (cockney rhyming slang)	pen and ink	stink
	mince pies	eyes
Midlands	fizzog	face
	mardy	grumpy
Cornwall (Cornish)	ha sos	hello
	dew genough	goodbye
Yorkshire	ey up	hello
	flibberty gibbet	person who talks too much

Glossary

accent	way words sound when people say them
capital	most important city in a country
coastline	edge of the land, where it meets the sea
curries	Indian dishes flavoured with herbs and spices
hedges	line of bushes around a field
mud flats	flat stretch of mud that usually leads to the sea
primary school	for children between 5 and 11 years old
rent	paying to live in someone else's house
sculptures	work of art shaped out of wood, stone or other things
semi-detached	house that is joined to another on one side
sightseeing	visiting interesting or beautiful places
stately homes	large houses surrounded by parks and gardens
terraced	houses that are joined together in a row
tourism	business to do with people visiting places on trips or holidays
traditional	something that has been done the same way for many years
uniform	clothes that people have to wear so they all look the same
worship	praising and saying prayers to something or someone

Index

The St George's Cross is the flag of England.